D1496579

AFTER THE STEAMING STOPS

POEMS BY

ALICE OSBORN

MAIN STREET RAG PUBLISHING COMPANY
CHARLOTTE, NORTH CAROLINA

Cover photograph courtesy of iStockPhoto.com,
    adapted for cover by M. Scott Douglass
Author's photo by Suzanne Hill, Zannelly Photography

Acknowledgments:

The author wishes to thank the following editors, journals, and books where these poems first appeared:

Iodine Poetry Journal: "Salt Marks," "Bad Cactus Blues"
Bay Leaves: "Ice Cream Party," "Featured Reader," "The
    Lesbians Next Door"
Broad River Review: "Early"
*The Best of Poetry Hickory Reading Series, a Main Street Rag
    Reading Series Anthology:* "March 30, 1981"
Dead Mule Southern School of Literature: "On Wearing
    Black," "King of Cool," "The Sentries," "Power Out"
Pinesong: "Duty after 'Nelson's Last Signal at Trafalgar'"
Yearbook (The Poetry Society of South Carolina): "Saturday
    Banking in Northern Virginia"

The author wishes to extend her gratitude to M. Scott Douglass, Scott Owens, Anthony S. Abbott, Jane K. Andrews, Beth Browne, Dr. Maria Rouphail, Judith Valerie, Sonia Usatch-Kuhn, Jan B. Parker, Juliet Patterson and Juliet's Poetry Exchange Group. To Keith, for his love and strength—always.

ISBN: 978-1-59948-353-5

Produced in the United States of America

Main Street Rag
PO Box 690100
Charlotte, NC 28227
www.MainStreetRag.com

For my family

Contents

SALT MARKS

My father didn't believe in air conditioning
on the May and August airless voyages
from college to home, home to college.
Cuts too much power!
No A/C in the Caddie,
between Southwestern Virginia to suburban D.C.,
over the Blue Ridge and woven valleys—
open windows conspiring with my father.

He smelled of Old Spice gone bad,
me of soggy grapes left out at a picnic.

When we arrived home to our columned porch
at the end of the winding private road,
my mother expected the white
diagonal marks crusting into my dad's
blue polo shirt and my favorite black sundress.

Didn't turn on the air conditioning,
again, did you?

She never said A/C—
my mother never shortened anything.

THE HISTORY OF PAINT

Drunk, my father
painted walls around the split level stairs
with White Dove OC-17.
Then he rolled a shiny gloss into
the rec room's brown paneling
to make it brighter and larger,
covering years of handprints, scratches,
kicks before we moved to other states.
What else does white hide?

Nothing was the same once inventors discovered
Charlton White, the first washable enamel,
conveniently available in tins for the man
of the house. Black marks
and sins erased thanks to the magic
of zinc oxide-based pigments.

Once I invited a date into my new apartment's kitchen,
handing him the merlot to open. He struggled
like a seal to open the cork, splashing
a pink polka dot cloud all over
the ceiling, fridge, laundry room door and floor.
I bought an Alabaster white for the occasion,
proud to cover up his mistake with a brush.
As if it were only that simple.

The Dutch revolutionized paint with oil,
the perfect binder using walnut extracts and lead oxide
to preserve wood from
weather, worms and wind. Never mind damage
to lungs and blood cells; the white lasted centuries.

My father doesn't paint his retirement house now—
all walls weakened by dog paws and cat scratches.
My mother doesn't want him to mess up again
or make the animals breathe in fumes.
I wonder if all he wants to do
is yank a brush, jam it
into the thick off-white paint
and roll-slap the acrylic until
only the tip of his nose remains pink.

NEIGHBOR ENVY

At eight I wished our neighbor
Mr. Scully was my father.
Perhaps he could replace a dad who drank beer
from his coffee mug
and tore my *Star Wars* Comic #48
into bits of Darth Vader and Princess Leia.
Mr. Scully had three teenage boys, saltwater fish
and Elaine, a quiet blonde wife who dressed in bright
polyester green and smelled like peppermint.
Unlike me, I bet Mr. Scully
never got harassed by the Safeway
recycling guy who believed we hosted
the wildest weekly parties.

Mr. Scully commuted to Honeywell
via blue Chevy wagon while my dad trudged
to the Metro bus shelter beside a Baptist church,
then trundled to the Pentagon subway station
to his government office on G Street, where he ate
a Snickers bar every day for lunch. Home at 7,
Dad would slump in his faux-Shaker chair,
gobbling up muenster cheese
on Ritz crackers while knocking down a Heineken.

What vices Mr. Scully had I could only guess,
perhaps he wore mismatched socks or didn't floss
nightly, maybe he told Elaine she shouldn't
go out in public with those emerald pants.
I can't imagine him nearly cutting off his thumb
while pruning the Christmas tree
on the red floored concrete patio, a beer resting nearby.

Would Mr. Scully have bought me toys at Kmart,
or gotten me a Egg McMuffin dripping gold
every time I'd visit his office downtown?
Dad and I watched two showings of *Tron*
to avoid a mother-raged home.

I discovered years later some fathers
excel more
at protecting than teaching.
Forgiveness is a selfish act.

ICE CREAM PARTY

Pale plaid dresses brush
against pink walls, patent leather
Mary Janes kick white tiles.
Two balloons escape into rafters,
and I haven't tasted even a teaspoon of ice cream.
I won't, not on this day.
My third birthday, high voices
squeal above the store's door chime.
Hands clap—my mother's—
demanding silence. Guests disappear
like popped bubbles. The girls go home
because I'm not behaving, my mother says.
I never find out what I did wrong,
but I remember her saying:
I love you, but sometimes I don't like you.

For a long time I feared the chance
of friends leaving early.
Will anyone love me when they know me?
Will they show up at my parties?
Now after a decade of marriage and two children,
I fear my tongue-sealed invitations
go unanswered. While cradling white wine
I don't want anyone to leave me.
I smile too wide, needy for crammed rooms.

BAD CACTUS BLUES

Every cactus craves water and sunshine,
but you'd say you don't need any of that nonsense.
Your soil stays sandy, a hint of dampness,
but never too much. You smell of fresh garlic,
on toast before it burns. You sprout
wide, filling up your shrunken pot
with roots scared of color, infiltrating
all corners of your territory. No other
succulent can compete with you since you
are always right and demand others
to share in your green, scalloped perfection.

Your needles grow long and venom-tipped.
When I enter the room you can't help
comment on my fat thighs, new
laugh lines and low class friends.
Plants are easier to raise than children.
I try to hug you but you don't want
my touch, perhaps your needles will break
and then who would you be?

ON WEARING BLACK

My mother told me once
I didn't deserve to wear white,
so now my closet is filled with black
pants, skirts, and tops—
a lacy collar pokes out
from my black lab coat.
Professional, practical.

Black pants absorb brick red
lipstick smashed into my cosmetic bay's
carpet when I bob to grab
a jar of miracle cream
for my customer in a shiny pink blouse
who'll return it tomorrow
at another store.

Getting ready for work on Sunday
I spot the velvet dress,
a cocktail number my mother
bought me at 17,
sight unseen my first college semester.
A snug size 6, she made me
promise I wouldn't gain weight before
the Homecoming Dance. Full of guilt,
its heavy matching coat
with draped embroidery hangs nearby.

She also told me I shouldn't sell
cosmetics, since I didn't know how
to touch people, as if tar sparks
would shoot out of my liquid eyeliner
and streak up a customer's hooded eyelids.
I wonder what she wore when she studied makeup
in Paris or if she was wearing black
the night she almost killed herself at 17.

MARCH 30, 1981

The news says someone shot our new president.
The same misty overcast sky outside our split level
that dampened my hair and Monday
reaches outside the Hilton's stone walls.
My mother rushes me to grab my ballet bag and shoes;
all I can think of is seeing that agent
in the pale raincoat on TV throwing Reagan
into the black limo with sweaty urgency.
I wonder if Dad knows him from work.

I whisper to the other eight-year-olds about Foster and Hinckley,
snatches of sound I grabbed earlier
like weeds, but none of them seem to care.
I'm distracted throughout my *barre pliés*
and can't wait till Mom picks me up
in our golden Granada for the latest news on the stray bullet.
Like me, Reagan wants to finish communism and heal
inflation, plus he doesn't go by a nickname like Jimmy.

On the ride home I warm to learn Reagan joked
about not ducking as he entered George Washington
on his own power—it's only twenty minutes away.
Hinckley shot off 6 rounds in 1.7 seconds,
striking four men. The length of a hand clap.
The President would be OK, but someone
named Brady remained in critical condition.
I want my dad to tell me more about the shooting,
but he adds nothing as he eats Ritz crackers
and drinks a Budweiser. *They were just doing their job.*
I'm afraid to ask more questions.

That night by the lamp I open my diary
with a brass key. Before my tiny red pencil
scratches the blue lines, I know
I don't want to be President or a Secret Service agent
at the mercy of a crazy person;
I don't want to die on a sidewalk.
Because my mother might read my words,
I write, *I went to ballet, it was cloudy
and the President was shot.*

SATURDAY NIGHT SOUFFLÉ

From memory my mother creates
a cheese soufflé, like the one Grandma made
before her daughter left France.
I'd rather do my algebra homework
but I'm so curious to see her fail.
Her voice is high and pinched;
might she sink the five egg ship?
She melts the butter in the iron saucepan,
and adds sifted flour until it turns golden like a crown.

Constantly stirring the roux clockwise
with a wire whip, she sprinkles in nutmeg and cayenne,
wiping spillage from tanned finger onto her full apron.
You'll mess the eggs up, she says,
so I grate a cup of Swiss cheese, cutting off
several slices for myself before setting
the dining room table, seldom used except
for bank holidays. I place four
white china plates from the sideboard and we'll eat
with the good silver she polished this morning.
She folds the egg whites into the ridged ramekin,
and for an hour proceeds to check her art
every fifteen minutes through the black-stained glass
where we've seen pound cakes rise and cookies flatten.

Like a cookbook picture, the soufflé is a chef's hat
newly ironed, tall and proud
to be alive. My brother complains
about not eating pizza as she sets the soufflé
on a trivet, the sides palpitating over the flowered

tablecloth, three pink roses brushing
against my stomach hungry for laced, burnt cheese.
My mother rushes back to the sink to clean
a pot or wash her hands, as my father
punctures the bubbling tower, forking
half of the soufflé onto his plate.
We stab the remaining carcass, leaving her
two tablespoons or less.
My mother screams at his rapacity—
she will never make another soufflé.

WHY I DON'T UNDERSTAND SNAKES

I don't understand why
in Mexico's ancient past
they worshipped Quetzalcoatl,
the serpent god of life
who wore a coat of many feathers.
In Egypt, Cleopatra's kin revered the asp's
poison—what a terrible way to die.

Aesculapius considered the skin
sacred, his cult let non-poisonous ones
patrol the sick bay floors;
but snakes don't heal anyone.
I touched a corn snake
at my son's birthday party
just to say I don't have
my mother's ophiophobia.
Batik rust and black patterns,
like a Taos Indian blanket:
it felt like an expensive French purse.

A long snake is an old snake
who has hidden under logs,
squeezed rats and frogs,
laid eggs and abandoned them
to flee before a hurricane's
pressure drop.

They thrive on independence,
no vegetarians among them,
even their brothers are fair game.

Mice enter the hinged jaws head first,
so the fur falls flat
as the belly juices digest every rodent drop.
Scientists now say most snakes
on Earth are venomous, even the pets.

We all have stories of a close encounter:
the black twig that moved,
the one on the path that almost
coiled around your leg,
the one who escaped in the fraternity house
or the one who found you in the bathroom
during your most private moment.

Maybe I'll never leave the Dark Ages
when a venom of serpents stood in
for the Devil, or the vampire:
sneaking into warm places,
trancing victims, stealing life.

FEATURED READER

Bree from Durham plants her feet a foot apart, her voice
a deep contralto. She's a warrior of words
at this weekly Charleston Open Mic show,
clutching her just-published red poetry book.
The emcee told her to get to the gig on time,
so here she is, gazing at only two filled seats.

Her poems ride on dark dragons with chainmail seats,
she plunges into images and coughs up a voice
without waver or worry, always taking her time
to debone and dethrone the excess weight of words.
At a writers' retreat in Asheville she produced a book;
her friends told her to Facebook and Tweet her show,

which hasn't really worked so far. But Bree shows
her captive diva in performances that usually fill seats
to Standing Room Only, selling at least 14 books
per gig. Her back of the room merch table possesses a voice
of ennui as the two audience members order coffee in loud words
and she prepares to deliver her best set in 20 minutes' time.

The door chime jingles. Five students rush in on Charleston time
and sit down with chair squeaks and their Open Mic show
notes. Bree repeats the first lines of her daffodil poem, the words
flutter, then fill like main sails. She looks up again, more seats
have jeans in them. She leans in towards the mic, her voice
thumping against the tan walls, thumbing pages in her book

gaining the lost page before they deny her the chance to book
her tour for her next collection, coming out in time
for Christmas. Five minutes left, she wills her voice
to rise and plummet like a child's bubble to show
them she can bring on the crowd, fill out of town seats
and make love to strangers with her words.

A few cars rumble down the cobblestones muffling her last words
as the emcee claps the audience to buy Bree's books.
Folks come in from outside, ready to fill up Open Mic seats.
They get recognition on Facebook with their five minute time.
One day several may even be a Bree from Durham with their own shows,
but they all better self-promote and Facebook their voices.

Bree finishes her show, takes her seat, clears her voice.
She wonders how many books she'll sell this time.

DUTY

after "Nelson's Last Signal at Trafalgar"

On one of our Sunday afternoon visits to Annapolis,
you wear your old white U.S. Navy shoes
while smoking your pipe.
You catch me staring at a sepia print
in your library, above the liquor cabinet.
Inside the rosewood frame
I see barefoot men in knee breeches and striped scarves
pulling the lines, waiting for a signal,
waiting for violet wind, waiting for something
grander than themselves.

My eyes train to the wigged man with small feet
wearing a tricorn hat standing next to two officers
on the ship's main stage. His empty right sleeve is stapled
to his black coat, heavy with medals.

That's Lord Nelson, Grandpa!
At eight, never had I felt so sure.
After all, I had just watched Nelson's story
on eight Sundays worth of *Masterpiece Theater.*
Yes, you're right.
Do you love me now because I recognize Nelson on the day he died?

Two decades later I learn Nelson told his men that day,
England expects every man will do his duty,
a saying all British children know like,
…ask what you can do for your country.
Your photogravure is worth less than an armchair,
hundreds once printed in a 1912 Christmas catalogue—
now it hangs on a single nail across my bed, four feet away.

I take it off the wall, blow the dust,
to absorb your cursive-print script on the back:
By Davidson, 1915, Kansas City, MO
framed in century-old yellow tape,
duty all you knew and trusted.
I waited a long time to know
your love was not conditional,
at attention only when we pleased you.
After you died, I secured our Nelson,
imagining your heart beating inside its glass lungs.

THE KING OF COOL LOOKS AT FIFTY

I idle my bike in this empty field,
dry as a Southern Baptist wedding.
I cough from the exhaust.
The scorched wildflowers on the edges
smell wasted, me on pot.
Don't smoke, don't drink anymore…
my body's given up way before telling me the score.

As a kid, I didn't remember my mother much,
and I never met my father.
He saw me as Josh Randall
on *Wanted: Dead or Alive*,
priming the "Mare's Leg,"
and never bothered to call.
Uncle Claude threw me
against walls on Sunday nights
after spending the day drinking Bushmills.
Saturday mornings he taught me
how to shoot rabbits and squirrels
in that shitty dump
I had to leave.

Mom showed up,
I couldn't stand her.
Hair dyed blonde, legs up in the air
men passed through her
like watches at a pawn shop.
At twelve, I was tumbleweed
that blew into Chino, the reform school
where I was never tall or strong enough,
yet hit hard without hurting my right hand.
(My first two wives would agree.)

When I made it in *The Magnificent Seven*
I asked Big Money to give
soap and jeans to the Chino boys.
Yeah, man, I worked my own stunts,
almost filmed me and not Bud jumping my bike
over the barbed-wire fence.
My dune buggy ride
made Ed Sullivan piss his pants.

They needed to know *I* drove the Mustang,
I always get the last word,
don't they know?
Maybe they could fail
but I couldn't.
When I die
it'll be front page news.

EARLY

I'm the last one he sees
before my train hits him
on a stretch between Cedar Rapids and Chicago.
His bark-brown eyes snap
in the inked jewel of gravel and air,
iron and wood,
damned and driver.

His loose body
ignores the descending crossing gates—
one hand extends a bottle,
the other clutches a Bible.
All of him whispers in the shallow pockets
of his leather jacket; he whips
his head around to face me. And I only hear
my mother saying, *It's better to be late
in this life than early in the next.*

A thousand parrots screech at once,
the whistle cancels him, his equation clears
off the books, debts repaid.

Later, his cracked rubber Rockports
mark the death spot.
In between the rails grows
a bed of yellow wildflowers.
He flew fifty feet
from the scored heels, the left tongue
bunched into the sweat-stained insole.

THE SENTRIES

Giant junipers kudzu our split level,
forming a perimeter around my mother's
manicured patches of tulips and hydrangeas.
The blue-green giants block out the sun
and the McKays' '76 wood-paneled
station wagon soaking up pollen and sap.
These privacy screens grow a foot
a year—my mother wishes
she could plant them along the sidewalk
so she'd never see others' weeds and poor
paint jobs: screw the codes and rules.

Trespass is possible thanks to a worn dirt chute
under the thick branches. The chewy buds sting and prick
one-kidneyed Danny McKay when he slithers
in his Catholic-school corduroy pants
onto the rooted ground and tumbles
head first into my front yard, two inches
from the magnolia tree bed.

My turn down the hill: on their side,
I feel the McKays' hard weed-grass on my bottom,
higher than my Traks sneakers from Kmart.
Danny can't help me when I scream;
I'm too weak anyway
to stop Jupiters fueled by manure.
The spiny needles attack me in the earth gutter,
under my shorts and socks.
I slide feet first, heel up the earth.
I'm spat out with red welts
that won't disappear.

MICRODISCECTOMY, CIRCA 2004

I

Rogue! You twisted tissue that loves to turn
inside my back & jump
into the soft jelly between
degenerated L-4 and L-5 discs.
Press, pulse & pound on the nerve root—
what fun to play outside the jelly mold.
You emerge from the bone spurs like a worm
after rain, smelling
of panic and dark earth.

II

You render me
stiff before prime time,
hard like Sunday morning
bagels on Tuesday.
I want to sleep the whole night,
(this fortnight of pain feels longer)
have full control over bowels & bladder.
Microwaved rice in a soft blue bag
gives up its loose position before dawn.

III

You'll make me end up like
the young old man in the square
who grips the back of the bench
with his left hand, shifts his weight
to his right foot & grips his
muddy brown cane in his right,
trudging forward at the end
of his downtown lunch hour.

IV

What is my attacker's color?
Could it be blue like
the waiting room?
Couches, bed rails,
blankets & scrubs.

Or maybe it's white like my nurse's hair
who dies a year later
from ovarian cancer.
The doctor saws your nasty tissue
& sews the taut skin
up into a clean lipline.
The oozing scar is a centipede
searching for a crumb on a
moonless night.
The pain is gone

but you remain a shadow—
I still hug
the headboard when rising
to meet my day.

POWER OUT

I

Wind whips the neighbor's oak leaves
into our front yard; early afternoon sky darkens
and I cancel the babysitter with a text—no driving tonight.
They say you can't see an East Coast tornado until it's too late,
the funnel hides in hail and stinging water hoses,
not like Kansas twisters, lone wolves in the prairie
touching down without a tear drop.

II

Last time I saw our son Daniel he rode his bike without his helmet,
skinny eight-year-old legs pumping down the sidewalk,
while his three-year-old sister slept on our green couch.
I'll find my own way! He likes to tell me, but not now
in this spring tornado I know he knows about
from watching warnings all morning.
Hail pings my Subaru from sponge clouds,
a tax from the global warming gods.

III

My husband's at work where rain invades the staircase.
He tells me the Sanford Lowe's is a ripped off sardine can
and I wonder if in my store manager days I would have
rushed customers away from broken glass and concrete.
Where's Daniel? I imagine his skull bashed by a mailbox
and his bike sailing over Oz, a helmet plunging
through a roof. But instead chills along my arm
tell me he's hunkered safe. Meanwhile, the power dies
and our daughter sleeps on.

IV

If you love someone let them go, but bar the doors
before a storm, no matter how much they complain.
A break in the rage and Daniel knocks on our door—
drenched, his new sneakers' purple laces strewn with bark
and burs. He followed a neighbor and her Chihuahuas back
to her house, no clue dueling cyclones ate children
near the road he and Daddy drive on everyday to school.

SATURDAY BANKING IN NORTHERN VIRGINIA

Yellow dust flickers in humid
air. I wear a white daisy shirt
like every Saturday when Dad and I
stop at the Giant, Hechinger's and First
Virginia Savings & Loan. I'm ten,
and hold fifty-seven dollars
in my account.

Dark cherry wood fills the space
and the bank ladies sit behind solid oak desks
where maroon carpet hushes our footsteps
and no one speaks above a whisper.

On the smooth table where the pens are lashed
I see a calendar with the date: Saturday,
April 13, 1983. Yellow buds
in a vase and a *Newsweek* at attention
"Gays in America" on the cover, two men
in red and teal holding hands outside.
They're a couple and there's no girl. I read
"Sex, Politics, and the Impact of AIDS."

Dad notices me staring; he says
nothing and I know that he *knows* I know,
but I don't know (not really). I gasp,
think it's my dad, but it's me.
What's outside should stay outside
and not enter a closet
where children give their money to kind lilac
women winking behind chained spectacles.

THE LESBIANS NEXT DOOR

I wondered if being gay was contagious,
if my parents would stop loving me
if I liked girls. I remember Dad saying,
It's good to have two kids,
just in case one is gay.

After the three women moved
into the raised ranch next door
they only allowed women to work on their house:
female plumbers, carpenters, and roofers.

Mom quickly sized up the roommates
before they unpacked their boxes.
She told me not to talk to them,
or to their yellow dog who had a different
name every Thursday. Mom and Dad whispered
about them every day, imagining their wild sex life
and I'd shut my ears when I'd catch on their lips,
Daughters of Sappho, the Isle of Lesbos, lesbian.

One drove a Jeep and worked for UPS,
another sunbathed in her orange bikini every Saturday
afternoon, and the fat one supplied groceries.
They all had short hair.

One night, I spied their big party
on their gray concrete patio from my
side window. My former PE teacher even came.
The women walked in and out of the sliding
glass door, beers in their hands, nodding

to the Pointer Sisters' "Jump for My Love"
and "I'm So Excited." Some hugged and kissed.
I stood on my twin bed, head tucked
like a turtle under my white roll-up shade,
eyelashes to the glass.
I wondered why the fat one
told them all to come in, later realizing
the streetlight cast a silhouette
of my ten-year-old head.

MOVIES WITH MY FATHER

I.

We head in different directions at the video store:
he to the rack filled with girls popping out of bikinis,
surrounded by men wrapped only in sheets,
and me to the sci-fi/fantasy section, hoping
for a long-awaited release of *Return of the Jedi*.
But no such luck. We meet in the middle
on neutral green carpet
where I can't believe he wants both
Spring Break III and *Hot Girls*.
No, Dad, not those. They're stupid movies, I say.
He tells me to shut up. *I'm in charge here, not you.*

II.

Dad takes me to the movies on Sunday summers,
and I pray there are no kissing scenes.
I'm sure the whole theater hears him whisper
Liplock, liplock! Can the girl break away
from Captain Kirk or Superman or Indiana Jones?
No one can cross lips again for the remaining
90 minutes! I poke around in the popcorn tub,
feel the kernels sticking to my back teeth.

AFTER THE STEAMING STOPS

As a young wife she hated ironing her husband's
shirts, steam stinging her eyes
as the collar, like butterfly wings, never folded down.
How the edges around the buttons puckered and puffed.

The cotton wrinkled as the stack of shirts
compounded in predawn light—she still had her own
skirts and blouses to iron, but these damn shirts!
As she poured more water into the steel-plated ship,
she thought about why she married him. Was it because
she missed her father? To get away from her mother and sister?
They could never lasso her back as a married woman
across gray seas to the tourist trap known as the French Riviera.

She wondered if she even loved him. He
was safety after the disappointments of dating combat
pilots who were every bit the cliché.
She wondered if she even wanted a family; he did.
Will three children be enough?
How would her body react to pulsating
red cells in her womb, the baby's fingers
are oak branches growing in a snowbound forest.

She tasted the starch, as she rubbed the iron
tip hard against the fabric, its clean scent
a hungry swallowtail moments
before it dies while sucking the life out of a zinnia.

AUGUST 31, 1997

Thanks to the front page,
I found out like most people:
how she lay dying in a Paris tunnel,
how the impact raked her in like soft hay in a baler.
With Binky the Siamese cat plopped on my lap,
I stop spreading strawberry jam on rye toast,
his skin folds and dusty white fur escaping over the print.
I wish he could lick all of that black type and spit up
a vicious hairball I'd shovel inside wet beach sand.

Loss reminds you about change,
and what you are willing to throw away.

One week later it's too early
for the calls of pelicans and egrets,
as I drive to a friend's home on Folly Beach
to view the prince-demanded funeral. I could
have watched at home, but her day demanded witnesses.
My boyfriend didn't know who she was
and couldn't understand her power.

It's the second time in 18 years
I've set my alarm to see such pageantry.
Eight horses carry the hearse
instead of the bridal carriage.
I cry more for her than I did
for any family death. I cry
for another death coming.

It's time for me to move out of his place,
tell him what he's afraid to say,
and take his fat cat and a few towels in the parting.